A COMPANION JOURNAL FOR
Satisfy My Thirsty Soul

My Worship
Journey

LINDA DILLOW

NAVPRESS®

BRINGING TRUTH TO LIFE

OUR GUARANTEE TO YOU

We believe so strongly in the message of our books that we are making this quality guarantee to you. If for any reason you are disappointed with the content of this book, return the title page to us with your name and address and we will refund to you the list price of the book. To help us serve you better, please briefly describe why you were disappointed. Mail your refund request to: NavPress, P.O. Box 35002, Colorado Springs, CO 80935.

The Navigators is an international Christian organization. Our mission is to advance the gospel of Jesus and His kingdom into the nations through spiritual generations of laborers living and discipling among the lost. We see a vital movement of the gospel, fueled by prevailing prayer, flowing freely through relational networks and out into the nations where workers for the kingdom are next door to everywhere.

NavPress is the publishing ministry of The Navigators. The mission of NavPress is to reach, disciple, and equip people to know Christ and make Him known by publishing life-related materials that are biblically rooted and culturally relevant. Our vision is to stimulate spiritual transformation through every product we publish.

FOR A FREE CATALOG OF NAVPRESS BOOKS & BIBLE STUDIES,
CALL 1-800-366-7788 (USA) OR 1-800-839-4769 (CANADA).

Introduction

Happy are those who hear the joyful call to worship, for they will walk in the light of your presence, Lord. They rejoice all day long in your wonderful reputation. They exult in your righteousness. You are their glorious strength. It pleases you to make us strong.

PSALM 89:15-17, NLT

Wonderful promises spill forth from Psalm 89. The verses declare that those who worship will walk in the light of God's presence. They will be filled with rejoicing over who God is all day long. They will delight in God's attributes and the Lord God will become their strength—not just ordinary strength, but *glorious* strength, because the Holy One delights to make His worshippers strong!

You hold in your hands *My Worship Journey,* a companion journal to *Satisfy My Thirsty Soul.* This is the third piece of the puzzle to encourage you to grow as a worshipper.

1. The book, *Satisfy My Thirsty Soul,* is an honest account of what I learned during my worship journey, combined with teaching and application to help you grow in living a lifestyle of worship.
2. The Bible study, located in the back of *Satisfy My Thirsty Soul,* takes you into Scripture so you can learn firsthand about worship. A major part of each Bible study lesson is a "worship experience" designed to enhance and deepen your understanding of worship.
3. This journal, *My Worship Journey,* is a place for you to record what you discover during the worship experiences.

Maybe you're saying, "If I am reading a book and doing a Bible study, why do I need to journal?" It is a good question. Let me try to answer it.

My Worship Journey not only acts as a historical record of your walk in the light of God's presence, it serves as a window into your soul. Your written words become an album of your thoughts, feelings, and experiences. As you chronicle, draw out, and reflect on who you are *becoming* as a worshipper, your worship experience will become more concrete.

The blank pages await you, not as a place to write pious prayers to God or to jot down what you think your Bible study leader wants to hear, but as a place for you to spill out your soul. Go ahead and stain the pages with your tears. Or doodle delightful pictures on the margins. This is your space, your place, where you can be real. That means:

- ❧ You can misspell.
- ❧ You can be sloppy.
- ❧ You can write what you really feel.
- ❧ You can be REAL.

The journal I kept during my adventure of growing as a worshipper is one of my most prized possessions, because it holds a part of me. I often pull my journal off my shelf and read through the pages. As I do, my heart leaps with joy. I can see how I've grown. I remember wonderful encounters with my Father. My reading turns to worship and prayer as I reflect on the joy of discovering God's voice and delighting in His presence.

In *Experiencing God* Henry Blackaby said, "If the God of the universe tells you something, you should write it down." I am so thankful I wrote down my journey. This is why I feel passionately about you doing the same. I believe your journal will become a safe place where you can observe, reflect, understand, and move toward change.

I am convinced that if you faithfully read *Satisfy My Thirsty Soul*, study God's Word, and journal about your worship journey, at the end of the twelve weeks you will say, "I have grown as a worshipper, and I am beginning to walk in the light of God's presence!"

Moses asked God to give the light of His presence for his journey to the Promised Land. God promised Moses that He would go with him. As you begin your journey, know that I am asking God to go with you and to be your ever-present Companion.

God's Blessings on your journey!

Linda Dillow

Journaling Tips

1. *Pray on paper.*
   Start with "Dear God" or "My Father" like you're writing a love letter to Him. Write straight from your heart the concerns uppermost on your mind. Instead of concluding with "Amen," sign it, "Your Loving Daughter, (and your name)."

2. *Sing on paper.*
   Allow your words to flow lyrically in unceasing fashion as David's words do in the Psalms.

3. *Think on paper.*
   Commit to embrace truth and reject lies about who God is and who you are.

4. *Feel on paper.*
   Be Real! Write: "I feel frustrated that writing is hard for me," or "Writing makes me feel good."

5. *Draw on paper.*
   Non-artists can express themselves on paper. Get some colored pencils or magic markers and give it a try! If you express yourself through art, the sky's the limit. Scrapbook, sculpt, paint, draw, use any medium.

6. *Document on paper.*
   Keep a record of what you have learned and how you have grown. Be sure to date each entry.

7. *Don't let perfection keep you from writing.*
   You aren't performing for anybody. This is *your* place to be real.

8. *Try a new place.*
   Discover a new location. Journal as you sit in the sun or hide under a tree.

9. *Record your emotions.*
   What is your dominant emotion this week? Anxiety? Joy? Hope? Write about it.

10. *Thank God for revealing new things to you.*
    Do you ever say, "It hit me" or "I suddenly realized as I wrote . . ."? These insights are gifts from God, so thank Him for giving them to you.

11. *Ask probing questions.*
    Ask the hard questions. You don't have to have answers.

12. *Thank God you are growing.*
    Detail new ways you are growing as a worshipper.

Week 1

—

My
Thirsty
Soul

My Thirsty Soul

O God, you are my God, earnestly I seek you; my soul thirsts for you, my body longs for you, in a dry and weary land where there is no water.

PSALM 63:1, NIV

I am excited that you have made the choice to go on your own worship journey! So much has changed in my life since I first began this journey:

- God's presence has become my portion.
- I am becoming a prayer warrior.
- My joy is unspeakable.
- I delight in intimacy with the Lord.

I was surprised to discover that God's presence is hidden in worship, and that as I grow in worship, I also grow in intimacy with the Lord. Worship begins in holy expectancy that we will see God, and it ends in holy obedience. It is the response of a lover to her Beloved; it is the lifestyle of a grateful heart.

We all long for *into-me-see* oneness with someone. Here is what Kathy told me:

I thought I would find deep intimacy in my marriage, but since my husband and I were both emotionally crippled for the first decade or so of our marriage, our relationship did not meet *my* expectations. I'd always searched for a soul mate, but felt that my husband wouldn't ever be that person. I craved someone . . . anyone . . . to be able to find me and know me to the core of my being. I longed for it and searched for it in Christian friendships. However, nothing and no one ever seemed to truly satisfy the deep need to "be known" so intimately.

The amazing news is that God intimately knows you and me, and He longs for us to know Him. The psalmist David said that the mighty God of the universe had searched and known him. God was intimately acquainted with all of David's ways (see Psalm 139:1,3). And the wonderful news is: your ways are completely known to Him as well.

A TEN-MINUTE
WORSHIP EXPERIENCE

It is time for your first worship experience. Four or five days this week, worship God by declaring WHO HE IS.

Here are some suggestions for your worship time:

1. Put on worship music, bow or fall to your knees, and be still in God's presence for ten minutes. Ask God to teach you about intimacy with Him.
2. As you kneel before Him, read Psalm 63:1-8 out loud to God. Ask Him to teach you about who He is and how you can grow in your worship of Him.
3. Declare all the truths you find about God in these verses. Here are four, continue reading and you'll find more.

   ❧ You are MY God.
   ❧ You are powerful.
   ❧ Your lovingkindness is better than life.
   ❧ I am satisfied with you—more satisfied than with chocolate (Linda's paraphrase).

Look at David's worship responses. Here are four to get you started.

   ❧ He thirsted and yearned for God.
   ❧ He saw God.
   ❧ His lips praised Him.
   ❧ He lifted his hands to God.

Write down in this journal what you thought or felt during your time of worship.

*One thing I have asked from the LORD, that I shall seek: that I may
dwell in the house of the LORD all the days of my life, to behold
the beauty of the LORD, and to meditate in His temple.*

— PSALM 27:4

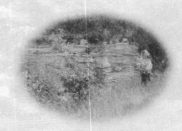

*How lovely are your dwelling places, O LORD of Hosts!
My soul longed and even yearned for the courts of the LORD;
my heart and my flesh sing for joy to the living God.*

— PSALM 84:1-2

*"Martha, Martha, you are worried and bothered about so many things;
but only one thing is necessary, for Mary has chosen the good part,
which shall not be taken away from her."*

LUKE 10:41-42

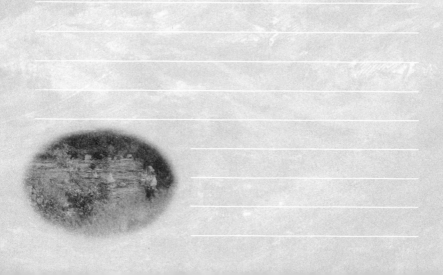

Prayer is the occupation of the soul with its needs. Praise is the occupation of the soul with its blessings. Worship is the occupation of the soul with God Himself.

"Lord, save my soul," is prayer. "Thank you, Lord, for saving my soul," is praise. "Thank you, Lord, for who you are," is worship. — A. P. GIBBS

It is important to be able to say, This is who I am. I am not primarily a worker for God. I am first and foremost a lover of God. All of us need to be lovers who work rather than workers who love. — BOB SORGE

Judy's paraphrase of Psalm 63:1-8:

O Lord, you are my Rock and my Redeemer. When my mouth is dry, I will drink of your Word. My body aches to feel your hug. Lord, I crave your love in a world that seems bone dry of your presence. I have known your intimacy in the secret place; I have beheld the power and glory of the King enthroned above. I long for your embrace and my mouth will ever speak of your love. In holy worship I lift my hands to the King; I will praise Him forever. My soul is like a vacuum filled only by your presence. My quivering voice sings praises to you and you are my last thought as I drift off to sleep. I dream of you, Lord, and then you are my first thought in the morning. Because I find safety in you, I wish only to stay in your embrace.

My worship journey has turned me from a Martha into a Mary. Does this mean I no longer serve others? No! I serve *more*, but my service now flows from a different place:

My service flows from a heart saturated with worship.

My service flows from a heart saturated with the presence of God.

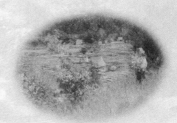

Worship is the upspring of a heart that has known the Father as a Giver, the Son as Savior, and the Holy Spirit as the indwelling Guest. —A. P. GIBBS

What did you learn about God this week?

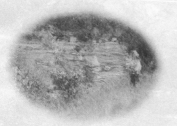

What did you learn about worship this week?

What did you learn about yourself this week?

_____

_____

_____

_____

_____

_____

_____

Write a prayer to God
expressing your hope for
your worship journey.

_____

_____

_____

_____

_____

_____

_____

_____

My
Worship
Awakening

❧

My Worship Awakening

*Holy, Holy, Holy is the LORD of Hosts,
the whole earth is full of His glory.*

ISAIAH 6:3

One woman said this about the beginning of her journey to become a worshipper:

> I saw a woman in worship. Her face was lifted to heaven, graced with a beautiful expression of joy. I thought, *What does she know that I don't know?* This began my search to know more of God and to become a woman of worship.

Like this woman I longed to wake up to worship. I was awake to God's Word but not to His voice and His presence. God opened my eyes and I began to grow in awe, astonished wonder, and adoration. I discovered that worship is to: *adore, admire, celebrate, esteem, exalt, glorify, love, magnify, praise, revere,* and *venerate* my holy God.

As I spent time on my knees in God's presence I realized that when I adore Him, worship becomes a beautiful and personal love exchange between my God and me.

God awakened me to worship! I pray He awakens you too.

THE ABCs OF WORSHIP

Worship God with the ABCs of worship several times this week. I love to let my mind free-flow and think of all my God is. As I move from A-Z, I become overwhelmed. Our God is an Awesome God!

Here are some ideas for this time:

1. Quiet your heart by listening to one or two worship songs.
2. Kneel, stand, or take a walk and declare to God all He is. Begin with the letter "A," and declare everything true of God that begins with "A." Then move on to the letter "B." If you need encouragement with the ABCs, look at Valerie's ABCs on page 37.
3. Write here about this worship time with God. What did you think, see, and feel? Was it hard, easy, or in-between?

_____

_____

_____

_____

_____

_____

_____

_____

_____

_____

In worship I acknowledge my limitations. In worship I also acknowledge that God has no limitations. I bow before Him. He is beyond me in everything.
— WATCHMAN NEE

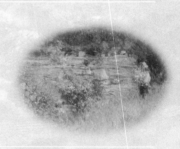

I will give thanks to the Lord with all my heart; I will tell of all Your wonders.
I will be glad and exult in You; I will sing praise to Your name, O Most High.

— PSALM 9:1-2

Worship is meant to be a love exchange between the bride of Christ and her beloved, Jesus. It's not optional; it's essential. In His glorious presence, every other competing voice is hushed to a whisper. — BECKY HARLING

To fall prostrate is beautifully reverent, blowing kisses is delightfully relational. — SANDI

We are under obligation to make our devotion to God so attractive that all who see us lost in the wonder of our praise might desire to know the object of our praise. — CALVIN MILLER

What did you learn about God this week?

_____

_____

_____

_____

_____

_____

_____

What did you learn about worship this week?

_____

_____

_____

_____

_____

_____

_____

_____

_____

_____

_____

What did you learn about yourself this week?

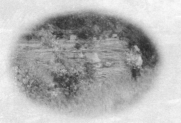

Write a prayer to God
expressing your desire to
wake up to worship.

VALERIE'S ABCs OF WORSHIP

A: Alpha, Architect of Life, Abounding in love, Angel Sender

B: Bountiful One, Banquet Host, Burden Lifter, Bondage Breaker

C: Chief Shepherd, Comforter, Compassionate One, Creator

D: Darkness Crusher, Death Defier, Defender, Deliverer

E: Encourager, Endurance Coach, Enthralled by my beauty

F: Forever Friend, Father, Fear Remover, Final Destination

G: Grace Provider, Gentle Whisperer, Glorious One

H: Healer of my body, Hand-Holder, Heart Restorer, Holy One

I: Invincible, Infirmity Eliminator, Immortal, Iniquity Eraser

J: Joy Giver, Jealous for my affection

K: Keeper of my heart, Kind King, Knows me

L: Light of the World, Lion of Judah, Life Giver, My complete Lover

M: Miracle Worker, Most High, Majesty, Music Composer

N: Never fails me, Never forsakes me, Nature Designer

O: Omega, Opportunity Giver, Overcoming One

P: Patience Provider, Peace Maker, Passover Lamb, Perfect Physician

Q: Quencher of my thirst, Quiets me with His love

R: Resplendent with light, Rejoices over me with singing

S: Super-Sized Super Hero, Salvation, Safe Haven, Shepherd, Shield

T: Trustworthy, Tear Wiper, Testifies in my favor

U: Unashamed of me, Unblemished, Understands me

V: Victorious One, Voice I long for, Valley Elevator

W: Wonderful Counselor, Wound Healer, Writes my name in heaven

X: Expert in all the ways of me

Y: Yahweh, Youth Restorer

Z: Zealous for His Holy Name, Zion Dweller

Week 3

———

My Soul
Finds
Stillness

My Soul Finds Stillness

Be still and know that I am God.

PSALM 46:10, NIV

Stillness brings a deeper understanding of God and His ways. My prayer for you this week is that you will become comfortable with stillness. Intimacy with God was the hidden treasure I discovered in stillness.

Begin your time with God by praying these heartfelt prayers:

Oh, my patient Father, the tyranny of the urgent seems so ever-present in my mind. As I kneel in your presence, I lay down my to-dos, should-dos, want-to-dos, and even can't-dos. But most of all, I bring you my fragmented mind with its swirl of questions and data and brokenness and demands and lay all, my mind, body, soul, emotions, and spirit, in rest at your feet. I lay this troubled head of mine on your knee and choose to look only in your face for this sweet time. Now, in this moment, there is only you. I love you, my Jesus. — SANDI

My Lord and my God, listening is hard for me. I do not exactly mean hard, for I understand that this is a matter of receiving rather than trying. What I mean is that I am so action oriented, so product driven, that doing is easier for me than being. I need your help if I am to be still and listen. I would like to try. I would like to learn how to sink down into the light of your presence until I can become comfortable in that posture. Help me to try now. — RICHARD FOSTER

THE TWENTY-MINUTE WORSHIP EXPERIENCE

I believe you will grow to appreciate the Twenty-Minute Worship Experience. Every day this week, be still before God for twenty minutes (if this seems like an impossibility, begin with ten minutes). If possible, be on your knees. (Yes, you can use a pillow!)

Here are some suggestions for your worship time:

1. Be honest: Tell God, "My Lord, I need you to teach me how to worship you."
2. Pray your Quiet Prayer.
3. Pray Psalm 131, asking God to reveal to you how your soul can be stilled.
4. Put on a headset and worship with worship music. Sing or say the music to your God.
5. Refer to the 365 Names, Titles, and Attributes of the Father, Son, and Holy Spirit on pages 157-159.
6. As you spend time on your knees before God each day, journal about what He reveals to you as you worship.

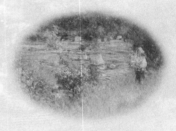

Surely I have composed and quieted my soul; like a weaned child rests
against his mother, my soul is like a weaned child within me.

— Psalm 131:2

When you pray, listen to the silence. Silence is a gift. There is power in silence. There is also a reverential fear of God in silence. Silence is a time to regroup, rethink, reevaluate, and reflect. Silence is the selah of God. Selah is God's musical interlude, pausing in the symphony of life to stop, look, listen, and take some time to think about what has been sung. In silence there is music, and God has a song. — PAT CHEN

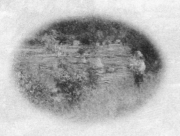

Busyness is the enemy of spirituality. It is essentially laziness. It is doing the easy thing instead of the hard thing. It is filling our time with our own actions instead of paying attention to God's actions. It is taking charge.
— EUGENE PETERSON

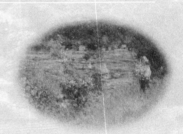

Learning to be quiet before the Lord is one of the greatest challenges we face today in our quest to enter in and experience true intimacy with Him.
— JAMES GOLL

My soul, wait in silence for God only, for my hope is from Him.
— PSALM 62:5

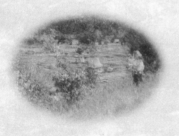

Rest. Rest. Rest in God's love. The only work you are required now to do is to give your most intense attention to His still, small voice within.
— MADAME JEANNE GUYON

I avoid stillness because stillness takes me to deeper places . . . places where I have pushed aside truths I did not want to face or believe . . . places where I have pushed hard things. Passion and pain live in still places. It takes courage to go to the place of stillness . . . courage and trust. I am afraid to go there. I approach worship with the same enthusiasm as exercise: If I can stay busy, I can avoid it. — AN HONEST WOMAN

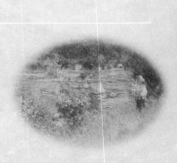

Though I am always in haste, I am never in a hurry because I never undertake more work than I can go through with calmness of spirit.
— JOHN WESLEY

What did you learn about God this week?

What did you learn about
worship this week?

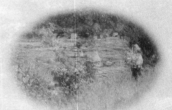

What did you learn about yourself this week?

Write a prayer to God
expressing how you long to
learn stillness before Him.

Expanding My Worship Experience

Expanding My Worship Experience

Come let us worship and bow down,
Let us bow our knees before God.

Are you ready to expand your worship experience? Adventure and excitement await you! As you go to your knees this week, ask God to stretch you.

If you do not visualize God as you worship, ask Him to give you a picture of who He is.

If you don't have a special place to worship, put your request in to your Father.

If you don't worship with special worship music that delights your soul, ask friends to share their favorites with you.

One honest woman asked God to set her free to worship Him. She said:

> I marveled at how, despite all odds, the Holy One could set Joni Eareckson Tada free to express her worship physically. I felt a great longing to be so free. It gave me hope that just as the Almighty could free Joni to worship fully beyond her physical paralysis, He can free me to move beyond my paralysis of soul that has so marked my worship. I wonder if Joni felt foolish and strange the first time she worshipped with her chair, but did it anyway, and then it became something free and freeing

to her. I am expecting that freedom. I am pursuing it. Joni represents my hope.

Augustine said, "God thirsts to be thirsted after." Go to Him thirsty this week, and He will satisfy your thirsty soul.

THE TWENTY-MINUTE WORSHIP EXPERIENCE

Again, this week I encourage you to practice the Twenty-Minute Worship Experience.

Every day this week, be still before God for twenty minutes. If possible, be on your knees.

Here are some suggestions for your worship time:

1. Be honest: Tell God, "My Lord, I need you to teach me how to worship you."
2. Pray Psalm 95, asking God to expand your worship experience.
3. Worship God with the ABCs of worship.
4. Put on a headset and worship with worship music. Sing or say the music to your God.
5. As you spend time on your knees before God each day, write in this journal about what God reveals to you.

Come, let's shout praises to GOD,
raise the roof for the Rock who saved us!
Let's march into his presence singing praises,
lifting the rafters with our hymns!

And why? Because GOD is the best,
High King over all the gods.
In one hand he holds deep caves and caverns,
in the other hand grasps the high mountains.
He made Ocean—he owns it!
His hands sculpted Earth!

So come, let us worship: bow before him,
on your knees before GOD, who made us!
Oh yes, he's our God,
and we're the people he pastures, the flock he feeds.

PSALM 95:1-7, MSG

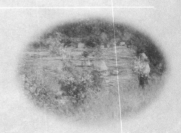

When I worship by the power of the Holy Spirit, the Old Testament melds with the New. Scripture flows into prayer and prayer flows into worship. Songs pierce my heart and love covers the wound. With the Holy Spirit as my guide, worship becomes revelation. — A WORSHIPPER

We don't need fasten-our-seatbelt signs in our pews because we no longer fly. We're like a group of geese attending meeting every Sunday where we talk passionately about flying and then get up and walk home. — TIM HANSEL

That's intimacy with God — to be so in tune with Him that no outward words or actions are necessary, only "pure adoration in spirit and in truth," from our spirit to His Spirit. — JAMES GOLL

Adoration is the spontaneous yearning of the heart to worship, honor, magnify, and bless God. In the prayer of adoration, we love God for himself, for his very being, for his radiant joy. — RICHARD FOSTER

Worship is the overflow of the heart that asks nothing of God.
— CARL ARMERDING

Worship is not a discipline that makes me stronger, wiser, more Christ-like. The purpose of worship is to know and be known; it is intimacy, communion with the Holy One. — KATHY

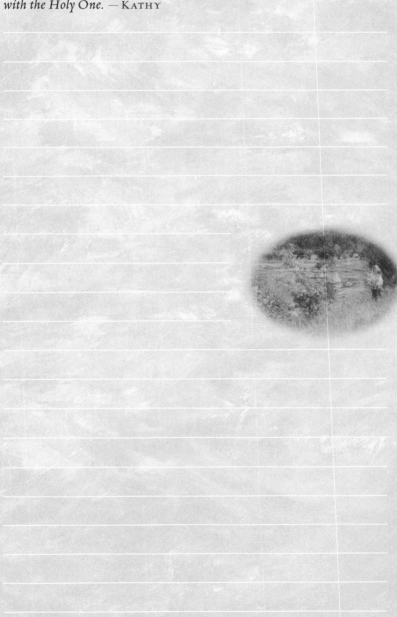

To worship in spirit is to worship spiritually.

A Christian should be an alleluia from head to foot. — SAINT AUGUSTINE

What did you learn about God this week?

What did you learn about worship this week?

What did you learn about yourself this week?

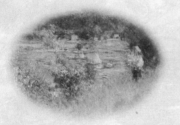

Write a prayer to God
expressing how you long to
grow in all it means to bow
your knees to Him.

I

Bow

My Life

⚘

I Bow My Life

Come let us worship and bow down,
Let us bow our lives before God.

Worship is the specific act of bowing my knees and declaring, "Holy, Holy, Holy." Worship is also a *lifestyle* of bowing my life and living "holy, holy, holy." Every day you and I have an opportunity and privilege to bow every area of our lives before our King. As I have lived out my worship, it has elevated my choices of obedience before my God. Truly, worship is the lifestyle of a grateful heart.

To worship is to respond; worship is the response of our heart to our Lover. What is my love response to the One who has given all? I can only bow before Him every day. I bow my life, my words, my attitude, my works, my times of waiting, my pain, and my will. But the foundation is that I first bow my life.

My friend Sandi expressed the surrender of Romans 12:1 like this:

I respond to your urgency Lord by laying down this body, soul, and spirit of mine, which in actuality is yours, but I acknowledge your ownership and release my claim, trusting in your mercy, and all you are. I offer this to you as what I can bring to your altar in worship . . . joyfully, expectantly, out of longing to make your heart glad.

My friend Kathy expressed her surrender in this way:

> When I at last gave my final percentages to God, I did the releasing from what felt like my grave. But losing the extra weight of that burden helped me crawl out of my pit and learn how to fully live! A life surrendered through crucifixion unto Jesus is a life fully resurrected by grace. Giving those final pieces of my old life hurt tremendously, but He wants all of me. The glory of God is a person fully alive, and I feel more alive than ever!

THE TWENTY-MINUTE WORSHIP EXPERIENCE

I hope falling to your knees and worshipping is becoming more comfortable for you. Again, I encourage you to practice the Twenty-Minute Worship Experience this week. Be still before God for twenty minutes every day. If possible, be on your knees.

Here are some suggestions for your worship time:

1. Be honest: Tell God, "My Lord, I need you to teach me how to worship you by bowing my life to you."
2. Pray Psalm 139, asking God to reveal insights to how He created you!
3. Take a "holy hike" and spontaneously worship God as you walk.
4. Put on a headset and worship with worship music. Sing or say the music to your God.
5. As you spend time on your knees before God each day, write down in this journal what God reveals about who He is and what surrender looks like for you.

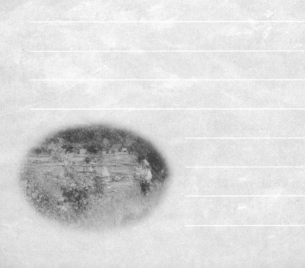

A summary of Psalm 25:14 and John 14:21:

> To fear my Lord is to obey Him;
> To obey my Lord is to worship Him;
> To worship my Lord is to surrender my All;
> To surrender my All is to love Him;
> To love my Lord is to be His friend;
> To be a friend of my Lord is to be His confidante;
> To be a confidante of my Lord is to share His secrets;
> To share the secrets of my Lord is to be intimate with Him.
> O how Amazing, how Incredible, how Inconceivable
> To have the privilege
>   The opportunity
>   The invitation
>   The ecstasy
>   Of such a relationship
> With the Almighty God of the Ages.
> How can it be that the unworthy be made so worthy
>   By One so Holy?
>
> — CHEE-HWA

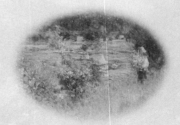

Obedience out of love is a doorway to more of Him. Worship draws us into an ever-deepening knowledge of His Being. Obedience draws us into an ever deepening understanding of His ways. Both are acts of love. Together they draw us into an ever-deepening love relationship with our Beloved.

— A WISE WOMAN

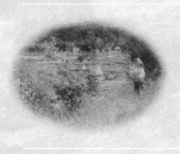

My heart I give Thee, eagerly and sincerely. — SEAL OF JOHN CALVIN

Worship is the submission of all our nature to God.
It is the quickening of conscience by His holiness,
The nourishment of mind with His truth,
The purifying of imagination by His beauty,
The opening of the heart to His love,
The surrender of will to His purpose,
And all this gathered up in adoration.

— WILLIAM TEMPLE

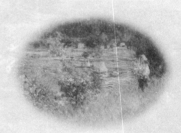

What can I give Him,
Poor as I am?
If I were a shepherd
I would bring a lamb.
If I were a Wise Man
I would do my part—
Yet what can I give Him,
Give my heart.

— CHRISTINA GEORGINA ROSSETTI

Worship is to be lived in the context of a 24/7 relationship to the Giver of all things. — A WORSHIPPER

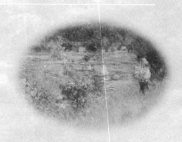

Look at all God has done for us! In light of the fact God gives us all and He is our all . . . is it too much for Him to ask us to offer our bodies as a sacrifice of worship? — A WISE WOMAN

If you obey my commands, you will remain in my love,
just as I have obeyed my Father's commands, and remain in his love.
— JOHN 15:10, NIV

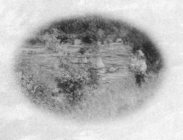

The secret (of the sweet, satisfying companionship) of the Lord have
they who fear (revere and worship) Him, and He will show them
His covenant and reveal to them its (deep inner) meaning.
— PSALM 25:14, AMP

I bow my life in worship and my life declares, "Holy, Holy, Holy!"

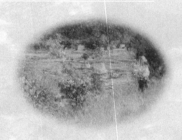

I don't have daily devotionals any more, I have "daily desperations!" I need the Word of God on an almost intravenous feeding plan.

— AN HONEST WOMAN

Where do I worship? Sometimes my mind is my place of worship and in the middle of everything, I just let my being worship. — SANDI

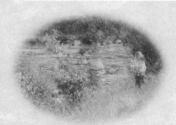

What did you learn about God this week?

What did you learn about
yourself this week?

What did you learn about worship this week?

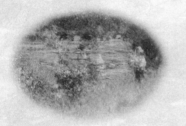

Write a prayer to God
about bowing your life
in worship.

—

I
Bow
My Words

I Bow My Words

Come let us worship and bow down,
Let us bow our words before God.

Our words have power—power for good or evil. A kind word picks up a person who is weighed down by trouble. One wise woman paraphrased Proverbs 18:21, which talks about our words, in this thought-provoking way.

> Our words are like vitamins or poison. When we speak kind, true, encouraging words, it's as if we give the people we are talking to very strong vitamins that make them have life and joy and energy. But, if we speak negative, harsh, unkind, untrue words, it's as if we are feeding them poison, and it results in their cells dying.

We have such a privilege—we can pour encouragement into those God has given us to love. And when we bless those made in God's image, we are also blessing Him. What joy!

My desire is that I never break God's heart with my words. I believe that this is your desire as well. May we grow to bless and encourage all those God brings along our path.

THE TWENTY-MINUTE WORSHIP EXPERIENCE

I hope falling to your knees and worshipping is becoming more and more encouraging to you. Again, I encourage you to practice the Twenty-Minute Worship Experience this week. Be still before Him for twenty minutes every day.

Here are some suggestions for your worship time:

1. Be honest: Tell God, "My Lord, I need you to teach me how to worship you with my words."
2. Pray Psalms 66 and 71.
3. Put on a headset and worship with worship music. Sing or say the music to your God.
4. Worship God wth 365 Names, Titles, and Attributes of the Father, Son, and Holy Spirit. (see pages 157-159)
5. As you spend time on your knees before God each day, write down what God reveals to you about who He is and about what bowing your words in worship looks like for you.

A gentle answer turns away wrath, but a harsh word stirs up anger. The tongue of the wise makes knowledge acceptable, but the mouth of fools spouts folly. A soothing tongue is a tree of life, but perversion in it crushes the spirit.

— PROVERBS 15:1,2,4

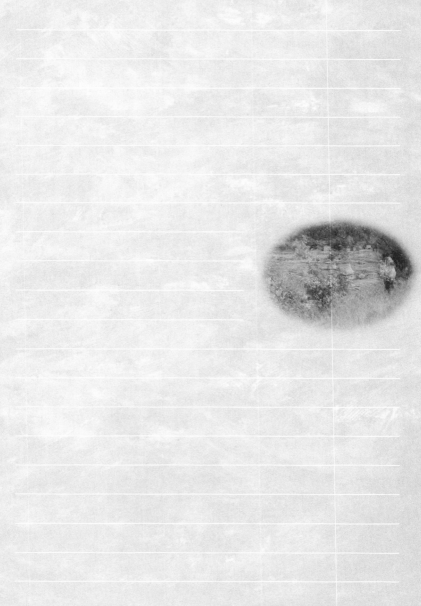

Death and life are in the power of the tongue,
and those who love it will eat its fruit.

— PROVERBS 18:21

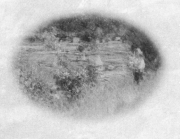

He who restrains his words has knowledge.

— PROVERBS 17:27

The heart of the wise instructs his mouth, and adds persuasiveness to his lips.
Pleasant words are a honeycomb, sweet to the soul and healing to the bones.

— PROVERBS 16:23-24

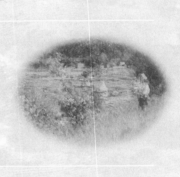

It is much wiser to choose what you say than to say what you choose.
The written word can be erased — not so with the spoken word.

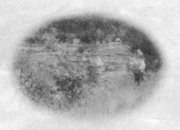

One of my definitions of worship is offering back to God as a sacrifice all the goodness and blessings He has given me. If I am pulling garbage out of my heart and spewing it forth, I certainly don't believe God would consider it worship. — KATHY

*God not only desires me to worship Him with beautiful words of praise —
that's easy — but He also desires me to worship Him with my words to others
as well. That one is HARD!* — BEV

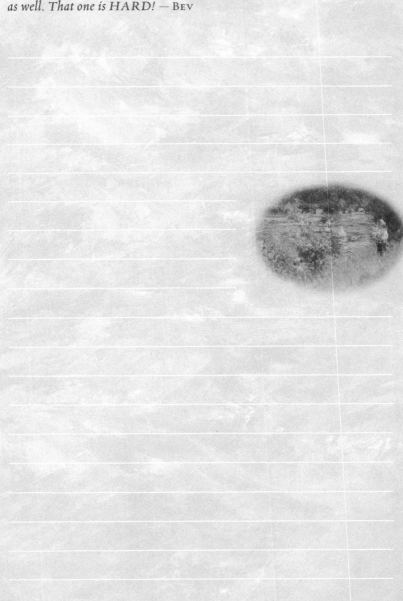

Like apples of gold in settings of silver is a word spoken in right circumstances.

— PROVERBS 25:11

It is better to live alone in a corner of an attic than
with a quarrelsome wife in a lovely home.

— PROVERBS 21:9, NLT

What did you learn about God this week?

_____

_____

_____

_____

_____

_____

_____

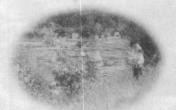

What did you learn about
yourself this week?

_____

_____

_____

_____

_____

_____

_____

_____

_____

_____

What did you learn about worship this week?

_____

_____

_____

_____

_____

Write a prayer to God about
how you long to bow
your words in worship.

_____

_____

_____

_____

_____

_____

_____

Week 7

—

I
Bow
My Attitude

I Bow My Attitude

Come let us worship and bow down,
Let us bow our attitude before God.

God's Word shouts from cover to cover, "Be a thankful people, let it become such a part of your being that you *overflow with thankfulness*" (Colossians 2:7, author's paraphrase). Gratitude to God should be as regular as our heartbeat.

Kathy expressed her desire to not have an attitude of grumbling, but an attitude of gratitude in the following prayer:

Lord, I want to live my life as a living sacrifice to you. When my attitude speaks more of my human nature than of my divine spirit, my sacrifice is tainted and once again this living sacrifice crawls off the altar. Continue to work on my attitude, Lord. May I be positive and encouraging in all situations, not just those seen in the open but especially in situations behind closed doors where no one else will see. Help me to continue to be a woman of integrity so that my personality and attitude reflect who you are at all times. My attitude is such a powerful witness of who you are in me. I pray I can worship you with an attitude of gratitude in all things.

Giving thanks in all things has to become a daily habit. It is not natural for our hearts to overflow with thanksgiving. Every day we must make a secret choice to give thanks. One woman expressed it like this:

I am just like the Israelites. I so easily go from rejoicing to despair. Gratitude is exactly like the manna God gave the Jews. It does not carry from one day to the next but must be "gathered" or chosen fresh each morning.

May we become daily gatherers of the attitude of gratitude!

THE TWENTY-MINUTE WORSHIP EXPERIENCE

I hope falling to your knees and worshipping is becoming more and more natural for you. Again, I encourage you to practice the Twenty-Minute Worship Experience this week. Be still before Him for twenty minutes every day.

Here are some suggestions for your worship time:

1. Be honest: Tell God, "My Lord, I need you to teach me how to worship you with my attitude."
2. Read prayerfully out loud Revelation 21.
3. Read Psalm 50 and meditate on it as you worship.
4. Put on a headset and worship with worship music. Sing or say the music to your God.
5. As you spend time on your knees before God each day, write down what God reveals to you about who He is and about what bowing your attitude in worship looks like for you.

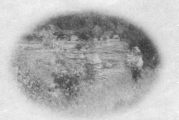

Our favorite attitude should be gratitude.

Gratitude is not only the greatest of virtues, but the parent of all the others.

Gratitude is an offering precious in the sight of God, and it is one that the poorest of us can make and be not poorer but richer for having made it.

— A. W. TOZER

No duty is more urgent than that of returning thanks. — SAINT AMBROSE

The most important prayer in the world is just two words long: "Thank you." — MEISTER ECKHART

The worship most acceptable to God comes from a thankful and cheerful heart. — PLUTARCH

Gratitude takes nothing for granted, is never unresponsive, is constantly awakening to new wonder, and to praise of the goodness of God.
— THOMAS MERTON

A smart woman said, "Being thankful gives me energy."

Reading the Psalms always moves me toward gratitude. Sometimes I have to read a psalm three or four times before I begin to agree with David in his gratitude. — AN HONEST WOMAN

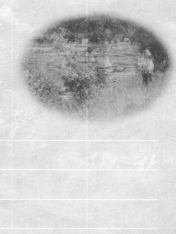

Attitude is the speaker of our present; it is the prophet of our future.
— JOHN C. MAXWELL

My Lord, how I long to live in constant acknowledgment of who you are by being always grateful. But ... sadly, I am weak and myopic. I yearn for this life of mine to be a dance of gratitude to you, my Beloved.

— ONE WOMAN'S PRAYER

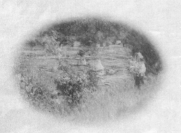

Giving a "sacrifice of praise" means emptying myself of my agenda and what I think is right for my day and instead seeing any detour in my plan as the gift of His plan." — A WISE WOMAN

The soul that gives thanks can find comfort in everything; the soul that complains can find comfort in nothing. — HANNAH WHITAL SMITH

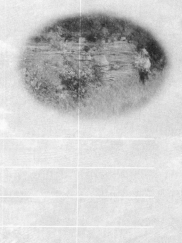

It's not so much what happens to us, as what happens in us that counts. — TIM HANSEL

Lord, can I be bold enough to thank you for hardship? Hearts molded in your refining fire will never be the same. I praise you for smoothing and softening my heart more and more every day into the image of the heart of Jesus. Lord, I praise you for holding hearts when they could have been shattered. My praise comes from a heart full of joy. All praise and glory and honor be to the One who knows everything about me . . . and loves me anyway. — One woman's Thankful Psalm

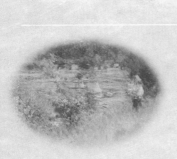

What did you learn about God this week?

_____

_____

_____

_____

_____

_____

_____

What did you learn about
yourself this week?

_____

_____

_____

_____

_____

_____

_____

_____

_____

_____

_____

What did you learn about worship this week?

Write a prayer to God
expressing how you desire
to bow your attitude
in worship.

Week 8

—

I
Bow
My Work

I Bow My Work

Come let us worship and bow down,
Let us bow our work before God.

It has been said that approximately half our waking hours are spent working. (Many women would laugh at this estimate—seven-eighths would be more like it!) In light of this, we would benefit from developing a new and higher view of work.

This Latin phrase gives us a new perspective of work: *Laborare est Orare. Orare est Laborare.* Translated it means, "To work is to worship. To worship is to work." How wonderful to see our creative *and* mundane work as an opportunity to bow in worship. Each of our moments of work, bowed before God, not only gives joy to others, but is counted as worship to the Holy One.

When asked how she described work and worship, one wise woman said:

What is worship? It is taking the part of my life called work and placing it on the altar as my offering to my God because I love Him. This is my spiritual act of worship.

May we live Colossians 3:23-24:

Whatever you do, do your work heartily, as for the Lord rather than for men, knowing that from the Lord you will receive the reward of the inheritance. It is the Lord Christ whom you serve.

THE TWENTY-MINUTE WORSHIP EXPERIENCE

I hope you are beginning to *want* to fall to your knees and worship. Again, I encourage you to practice the Twenty-Minute Worship Experience this week. Be still before Him for twenty minutes every day.

Here are some suggestions for your worship time:

1. Be honest: Tell God, "My Lord, I need you to teach me how to worship you with my work."
2. Meditate in your worship time on Psalm 90; Psalm 5; and Psalm 16.
3. Worship with the ABCs of worship.
4. Put on a headset and worship with worship music. Sing or say the music to your God.
5. As you spend time on your knees before God each day, write down what God reveals to you about who He is and about what it looks like for you to bow your work in worship.

When physical, mundane work seems tedious, remember: God did physical labor. He created the world out of nothing, but also planted a garden (Genesis 2:8-9), heaved the giant door of Noah's ark shut, (Genesis 7:16), and even acted as a cook (Psalm 104:27-28)! The only thing we know about the Lord Jesus from ages twelve to thirty is that he worked with his hands as a carpenter. This was his "spiritual" preparation for ministry.

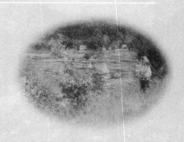

*"I have brought you glory on the earth by completing
the work that you gave me to do."*
— JOHN 17:3, NIV

*Before this study I believed that sitting at the feet of Jesus was spiritual and
that preparing meals was not. Now I see that EVERYTHING I do can be
an offering to the Lord.* — BEV

Work is worship;
God, my brother,
Takes our toils for homage sweet
And accepts as signs of worship
Well worn hands and wearied feet.
— THOMAS W. HANDFORD

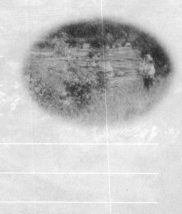

Oswald Chambers had this beautiful thought about our work: We are to
worship, wait, and then work.

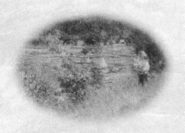

Brother Lawrence had it figured out. He knew who he was working for. "That we ought not to be weary of doing little things for the love of God, who regards not the greatness of the work, but the love with which it is performed."

A MOTHER'S PRAYER

My Lord, so much of being a mother at home is servant's work. It requires no special skill and it never ends. Working outside the home was so much easier. But Lord, I accept your assignment. I bow my cleaning to you as my daily act of worship. You—not my husband nor my children — are my employer. Your favor and presence is my reward. I invite you into my work of service toward my family, not just in the teachable moments of mothering, but in the daily work of creating a haven for my loved ones. I worship you under the kitchen table as I clean up crumbs, I worship you as I potty train, help with homework, feed hungry children, and teach my son not to bite his sister. I worship you in this "work" because it has all been assigned by you.

— CHEE-HWA

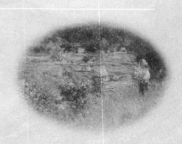

What did you learn about God this week?

What did you learn about yourself this week?

What did you learn about worship this week?

Write a prayer to God
expressing how you
long to bow your work
in worship.

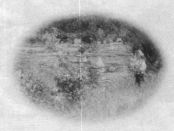

I Bow
My Times
of Waiting

I Bow My Times of Waiting

Come let us worship and bow down,
Let us bow our times of waiting before God.

Waiting on God is one of the most difficult things we will ever be asked to do. We don't know how long we will have to wait or how difficult the time of waiting will be. What do we do during these hard times?

Eugene Peterson says, "Waiting does not mean doing nothing. It is not fatalistic resignation. It means going about our assigned tasks, confident that God will provide the meaning and the conclusion. It is not compelled to work away at keeping up appearances with a bogus spirituality. It is the opposite of desperate and panicky manipulations, of scurrying and worrying."

The following prayer shows how one wise woman is bowing her times of waiting:

> Lover of my soul, I embrace your timetable, not only what happens but also the speed or lack of it, in which you choose to make things happen. You will do only good and if there were any better way than waiting, you'd do that, but I accept waiting as your gift to me and release my need for an answer NOW or even ever. I relinquish my "right" to a speedy answer and rest in the certainty that your great love for me means this time of waiting is best. Have your way, in your time, my Jesus and I will always simply be yours.

THE TWENTY-MINUTE WORSHIP EXPERIENCE

For eight weeks, you have been participating in worship experiences. I hope it is more natural now for you to be on your knees or on a walk worshipping the Holy One.

Again, I encourage you to practice the Twenty-Minute Worship Experience this week. Be still before Him for twenty minutes every day.

Here are some suggestions for your worship time:

1. Be honest: Tell God, "My Lord, I need you to teach me how to worship you with my times of waiting."
2. Worship God with all the names of God the Father, God the Son, and God the Spirit that you can bring to mind.
3. Meditate in your worship time on Psalm 31 and Psalm 18.
4. Put on a headset and worship with worship music. Sing or say the music to your God.
5. As you spend time on your knees before God each day, write in this journal about what God reveals to you about who He is and what bowing your times of waiting in worship looks like for you.

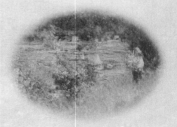

I sensed the Lord saying to me, "My daughter, until it's time, it's not time. Can you trust me?" I get this picture of a cake taken out of the oven before it's fully cooked. It is ugly and runny, and you just can't eat it. The point isn't how long I wait, it's that in God's timetable it's not time yet. Like the cake, I'm not ready—and I really don't want Him to pull my dreams and plans out of the oven before they're fully cooked. — SANDI

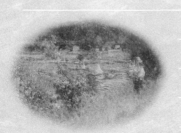

Quiet waiting before God would save from many a mistake and from many a sorrow. — JAMES HUDSON TAYLOR

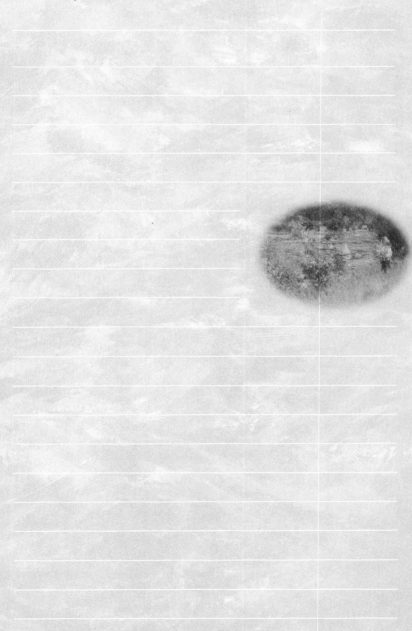

I wait quietly before God, for my victory comes from him. He alone is my rock and my salvation, my fortress where I will never be shaken. Let all that I am wait quietly before God, for my hope is in him.
— PSALM 62:1-2, 5, NLT

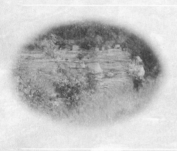

I am beginning to see that "waiting" is one of my Father's greatest gifts to me. He loves me enough to have me wait so that in the waiting I can discover greater intimacy with Him. — A WISE WOMAN

But as for me, I trust in You, O LORD, I say, "You are my God."
My times are in Your hand.
— PSALM 31:14-15

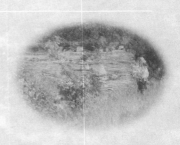

Almost every day this week I have woken up dry and empty . . . and every
day as I worship, whether in the Twenty-Minute Worship Experience
or in bowing my work or attitude or times of waiting or whatever, God
has met me and been real. While my mind knows He is always there,
worship causes my mind, spirit, and soul to truly know it and be at rest.
— A WOMAN GROWING IN WORSHIP

I want to trust like David, but it often takes me a lot longer than ten or fifteen verses to get to, "But I trust in you." Many of my waitings are still in process. — AN HONEST WOMAN

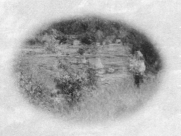

My Abba, I'm sorry that I fight and wrestle with you so much of the time. I want to be healed yesterday—in fact, I wish I'd never been abused. I am so tired and I feel sick inside, but I submit my hopes and dreams to you, and I trust your timing." — ONE WOMAN'S PRAYER

God may seem slow, but he's never late. — ROY LESSIN

Be strong and let your heart take courage, all you that wait for the Lord.

— PSALM 31:24

What did you learn about God this week?

What did you learn about yourself this week?

What did you learn about worship this week?

Write a prayer to God
expressing how you are
going to bow your times
of waiting.

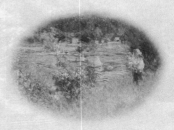

Week 10

—

I

Bow

My Pain

❧

I Bow My Pain

Come let us worship and bow down,
Let us bow our pain before God.

A man once drew some black dots. No one could make anything of them but an irregular assemblage of black dots. Then he drew a few lines, put in a few rests, then a clef at the beginning, and it became clear that the black dots were musical notes for the doxology:

> Praise God from whom all blessings flow,
> Praise Him all creatures here below.

Each of us has many black dots and black spots in our lives. We cannot understand *why* they are there or *why* God permitted them to come. But if we let Him adjust the dots in the proper way, draw the lines He wants, and put in the rests at the appropriate places, then out of the black dots and spots in our lives He will make a glorious harmony.

When I bow my pain, it is an act of worship. "But as for me, I *will* hope continually, and *will* praise you yet more and more!" (Psalm 71:14, emphasis added). Praise in our prisons of pain is a high form of worship. As C. H. Spurgeon says, "Our grief cannot mar the melody of our praise, it is simply the bass notes of our life song, 'To God Be the Glory.' "

May we grow in bowing our pain in worship so our life song will become "To God Be the Glory!"

THE TWENTY-MINUTE WORSHIP EXPERIENCE

Is worship beginning to be part of your life? I hope so! Again, I encourage you to practice the Twenty-Minute Worship Experience this week. Be still before Him for twenty minutes every day.

Here are some suggestions for your worship time:

1. Be honest: Tell God, "My Lord, I need you to teach me how to worship you in my pain."
2. Meditate and personalize Psalm 20.
3. Read aloud and pray Psalm 142 to God.
4. Read Psalm 27 and pray it personally to God.
5. Put on a headset and worship with worship music. Sing or say the music to your God.
6. As you spend time on your knees before God each day, write down what God reveals to you about who He is and about what it looks like for you to bow your pain in worship. Be honest and tell Him how hard it is to bow your pain.

_____

_____

_____

_____

_____

_____

_____

_____

_____

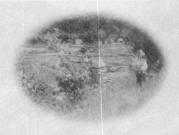

The pain of rejection and abandonment cause me to feel unloved and lonely, but God is using it to make me desperate for Him. He is coming to me in worship and the walls of fear and distrust are coming down in His presence.
— AN HONEST WOMAN

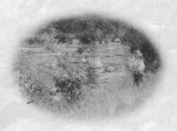

Afflictions are but the shadow of God's wings. — GEORGE MACDONALD

He said not: thou shalt not be troubled, thou shalt not be tempted, thou shalt not be distressed. But he said thou shalt not be overcome.
— JULIAN OF NORWICH

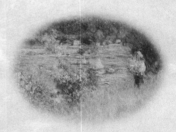

Sorrow is a fruit; God does not allow it to grow on a branch that is too weak to bear it. — VICTOR HUGO

When you are in the dark, listen, and God will give you a very precious message for someone else when you get into the light. — OSWALD CHAMBERS

When one loves what God is doing in one's life, one cannot hate the instrument through which it comes. — MADAME JEANNE GUYON

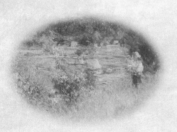

When you find yourself in the midst of pain, begin to worship God. As we worship the Lord, the atmosphere is changed. When Paul and Silas were in jail, their songs of worship became a weapon against the enemy and the doors of their prison were opened wide.

For in the day of trouble He will conceal me in His tabernacle;
in the secret place of His tent He will hide me.

— PSALM 27:5

Thank the good God for having visited you through suffering; if we knew the value of suffering, we would ask for it. — BROTHER ANDREW

Never judge God by suffering, but judge suffering by the cross.
— FATHER ANDREW

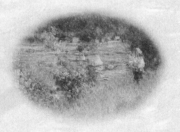

Have courage for the great sorrows of life, and patience for the small ones. And when you have laboriously accomplished your daily task, go to sleep in peace. God is awake. — VICTOR HUGO

For You light my lamp; the LORD my God illumines my darkness.
For by You I can run upon a troop; and by my God I can leap over a wall.
— PSALM 18:28-29

The Lord is a shelter for the oppressed, a refuge in times of trouble.
— PSALM 9:9, NLT

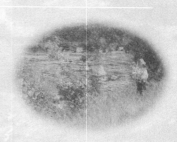

A season of suffering is a small price to pay for a clear view of God.
— MAX LUCADO

God is our refuge and strength, a very present help in trouble.
Therefore we will not fear.
— PSALM 46:1-2

What did you learn about God this week?

_____

_____

_____

_____

_____

_____

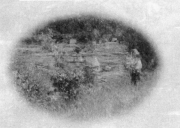

What did you learn about
yourself this week?

_____

_____

_____

_____

_____

_____

_____

_____

What did you learn about worship this week?

Write an honest prayer
about the "pain" of bowing
your pain to God.

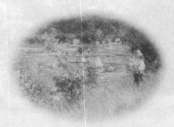

Week 11

—

I
Bow
My Will

I Bow My Will

Come let us worship and bow down,
Let us bow our will before God.

A woman asked me, "Linda, what is the deepest form of worship?"

I answered, "It is what Jesus did in the Garden of Gethsemane. With great physical anguish and agony of spirit, Jesus bowed His will to God's will. His words resound through the centuries as the deepest act of worship, 'Going a little farther, he fell with his face to the ground and prayed, "My Father, if it is possible, may this cup be taken from me. Yet not as I will but as you will"' (Matthew 26:39, NIV)." A woman growing as a worshipper said she loved this verse for two reasons:

1. "Going a little farther." This is the Scripture of "farther still." Jesus wanted His friends to help Him in His time of anguish, but He had to go beyond the help of Peter, John, and James. I can picture Him crawling "farther still" until He was lying at the feet of His Father in anguish. The place of "farther still" is a place beyond where anyone on earth can help us. To gain true comfort it is often necessary to "bloody" our knees to get there.

2. "Yet not as I will but as you will." Ahh . . . relinquishment. God, take away this pain, but if it must remain mine, let me live with your grace. Jesus fell into the peace of His Father's will even though He knew it meant chaos and crucifixion. This Scripture is exactly what bowing in worship is all about . . . falling into the peace of the Father and knowing the intimacy

of His presence, even though chaos may surround me. This is the kind of surrendered life I long to live.

It is wrenching to name our "Isaac" and lay him on the altar. When we go through our "personal garden experiences" and bow our will to the Father's will, God delights, the angels sing, and all heaven rejoices. In relinquishing our will to God's will, the peace of God's soft presence is found.

THE TWENTY-MINUTE WORSHIP EXPERIENCE

Like Jesus, when you face bowing your will to the Father's will, it will be a "falling on your knees" time. As you spend your twenty minutes before the Lord each day this week, ask Him to take you deeper in all it means to bow your will to Him.

Here are some suggestions for your worship time:

1. Be honest: Tell God, "My Lord, I need you to teach me how to bow my will in worship. "
2. Worship God with the ABCs of Worship (to refresh your memory, refer to chapter 2).
3. Worship God with Psalm 91; Psalm 40; and Psalm 84.
4. Put on a headset and worship with worship music. Sing or say the music to your God.
5. As you spend time on your knees before God each day, write down what God reveals to you about who He is and about what it looks like for you to bow your will. Be honest—write the "good and the bad."

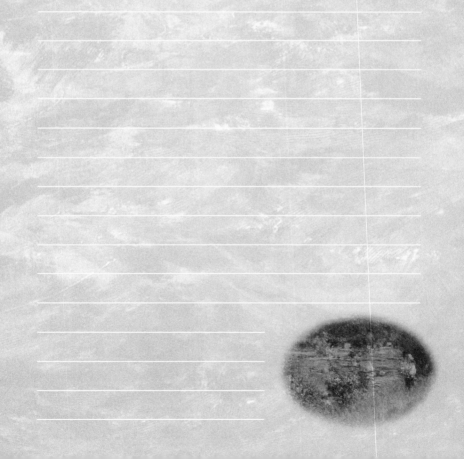

True heart sacrifice involves:

- ❧ *Identifying something precious to us (our Isaac).*
- ❧ *Letting go of our control over the situation, event, or the person as an act of worship.*
- ❧ *Resting in the outcome, even if in this lifetime we are not allowed to understand the reason behind the need for the sacrifice and the pain involved.*

— Carol Kent

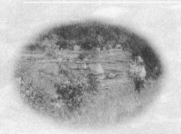

Doing the will of God leaves me no time for disputing his plans.
— George MacDonald

This week I have come to believe that when laying anything down that embodies my "Isaac," I ultimately must also bring pieces of myself before the altar. I bring my insecurities, my comfort, my love, my joy, my fears, my personality, my control, my manipulation — all are wrapped up in whatever my Isaac is. — AN HONEST WOMAN

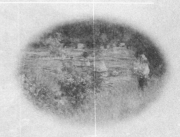

God, grant me the serenity to accept the things I cannot change, courage to change the things I can, and wisdom to know the difference, living one day at a time, enjoying one moment at a time, accepting hardship as a pathway to peace, taking, as Jesus did, this sinful world as it is, not as I would have it, trusting that You will make all things right if I surrender to Your will, so that I may be reasonable happy in this life and supremely happy with You forever in the next. — REINHOLD NIEBUHR

Blessed is he who submits to the will of God; he can never be unhappy. — MARTIN LUTHER

There are no disappointments to those whose wills are buried in the will of God. — FREDERICK WILLIAM FABER

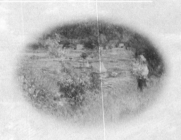

Ascertaining God's will is often a painful and heart-searching experience, mainly because most of us have an inner reluctance to do the will of God without reservation. — J. OSWALD SANDERS

The center of God's will is our only safety. — BETSIE TEN BOOM

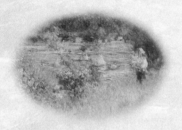

God of all goodness, grant us to desire ardently, to seek wisely, to know surely and to accomplish perfectly thy holy will, for the glory of thy name.
— THOMAS AQUINAS

O Lord, Thou knowest that which is best for us. Let this or that be done, as thou shalt please. Give what thou wilt, how much thou wilt, and when thou wilt. — THOMAS Á KEMPIS

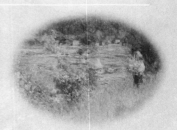

What did you learn about God this week?

What did you learn about yourself this week?

What did you learn about worship this week?

Write a prayer expressing
your hope of bowing
your will in worship.

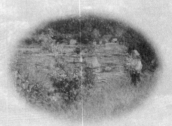

Week 12

Drawn into
His Presence

Drawn into His Presence

*For He has satisfied the thirsty soul,
and the hungry soul He has filled with what is good.*

PSALM 107:9

While we are at the end of this book, I hope this will not be the end, but the beginning of a lifelong worship journey for you! When we started, I said that worship begins in holy expectancy and ends in holy obedience. I also told you that hidden in worship is the presence of God.

I asked my friend Lorraine to tell you how she discovered God's presence.

How did I come to this place of knowing His Presence?

At first, there was much effort. Like a hidden treasure, I searched Him out, pursuing every clue that would lead me to Him. I moved rocks and dirt, dug deep in God's Word, and attended every Bible study or conference that would reveal Him. God often rewarded my searching with precious nuggets and gems, but I knew that I had not yet found the whole of the treasure.

About ten years into the hunt, something changed. Almost imperceptibly, I became aware that my labor was no longer needed—that the treasure was not a destination, but God Himself. Daily, He brought the treasure of His Presence to me. Labor ceased. We simply enjoyed each other. Sometimes we shared the depths of comfort and laughter that is shared between lifelong friends. Other times we shared the passions and dreams of two intimate lovers. Still other times, it was the excitement of discovery as an all-wise teacher revealed hidden secrets to an eager student.

He has become all things to me: Father, Friend. Lover, Teacher. Companion, Holy Ruler. I am as comfortable bowing down to Him in fear and trembling as I am snuggling in His arms.

He is the breath in my lungs, the blood in my veins, the passion of my heart, and the fulfillment of all my longings.

The Twenty-Minute Worship Experience

This is the last week of our worship journey together, but I hope for you it is only the beginning of a lifetime of worship!

This week I would like you to look back. Spend time looking through each week of *My Worship Journey*.

Each day during your Twenty-Minute Worship Experience thank God for all He has taught you about Himself, all you have learned about YOU and about worship.

Here are other suggestions for your worship time:

1. Be honest: Tell God, "My Lord, I want to go deeper in knowing your presence."
2. Worship God with Psalm 16, Psalm 89, and Psalm 42.
3. Put on a headset and worship with worship music. Sing or say the music to your God.

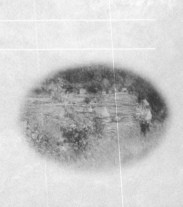

The beauty of bowing everything as an act of worship is that we discover His presence in the most mundane of places (like writing an e-mail or pruning roses). I love this! My life can become my love song to Jesus!
— A WORSHIPPER

By dwelling in the presence of God, I have established such a sweet communion with the Lord that my spirit abides, without much effort, in the restful peace of God. In this rest, I am filled with faith that equips me to handle anything that comes to me. — BROTHER LAWRENCE

> *Happy are those who hear the joyful call to worship,*
> *for they will walk in the light of your presence.*
> — PSALM 89:15, NLT

Over the last ten years, I have chased after His presence with all my strength.
As I have chosen to run to Him rather than running away from Him, I have
experienced a far deeper intimacy with Him than I had ever imagined. How
have I done this? Through practicing His presence and making worship a
priority. — BECKY HARLING

And the four living creatures, each one of them having six wings,
are full of eyes around and within; and day and night they do not cease to say,
"HOLY, HOLY, HOLY IS THE LORD GOD, THE ALMIGHTY,
WHO WAS AND WHO IS AND WHO IS TO COME."
— REVELATION 4:8

The Spirit and the bride say, "Come." And let the one who hears say,
"Come." And let the one who is thirsty come; let the one who
wishes take the water of life without cost.
— REVELATION 22:17

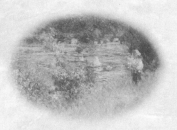

Often someone who knows the Lord intimately will make us painfully
hungry for a higher and deeper experience of Christ. It is the greatest
of all influences, to provoke another believer to thirst as a deer after the
waterbrook.

God is more real to me than any thought or thing or person. I feel Him in the sunshine or rain. I talk to Him as to a companion. I pray and praise, and our communion is delightful. He answers me again and again, often in words so clearly spoken that it seems my outer ear must have carried the tone, but generally in strong mental impressions. He speaks to me through the Scripture and unfolds some new view of Him and His love for me. The truth that He is mine and I am His never leaves me; it is an abiding joy.
— WILLIAM JAMES

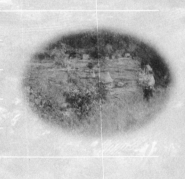

I have only begun to grow as a worshipper. I thought I knew about worship, but this pursuit will take my whole life. Worship is what I was made for, what each of us were made for. — A WISE WOMAN

Then I looked, and I heard the voice of many angels around the throne and the living creatures and the elders; and the number of them was myriads of myriads, and thousands of thousands, saying with a loud voice, "Worthy is the Lamb that was slain to receive power and riches and wisdom and might and honor and glory and blessing."
— REVELATION 5:11-12

What did you learn about God this week?

What did you learn about yourself this week?

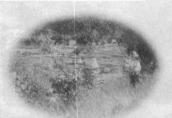

What did you learn about worship this week?

Write a prayer to God about
how you long to continue to
grow as a worshipper and
walk in His presence.

365 Names, Titles, and Attributes of the Father, Son, and Holy Spirit

Abba, Father
Abiding
Able
Abounding and Abundant
Adequacy
Adonai, Lord and Master
Advocate
All
All-knowing
Almighty God
Alpha and Omega
Amen
Ancient of Days
Anointed of God
Answer
Architect and Builder
Arm of the Lord
Ascended
Atonement
Author and Finisher of
 Faith
Authority
Available
Avenger
Awesome
Balm of Gilead
Banner to the People
Beautiful
Before All Things
Beginning and End
Beloved Son of God
Betrothed
Blameless
Blessed Hope
Blesses
Bread from Heaven
Bread of Life
Bridegroom
Bright Morning Star
Brightness of Glory of God
Brother
Burden-bearer
Captain of the Lord's Host
Carpenter

Chief Cornerstone
Chief Shepherd
Child Jesus
Choice and Precious
Chosen of God
Christ Jesus our Lord
Christ the Power of God
Cleansing
Comforter
Coming Again
Commander of the Army
 of the Lord
Compassionate
Complete
Confidence
Conquering
Consolation
Consuming fire
Counselor
Covenant-keeping God
Cover for Sin
Creator
Crucified
Defender and Defense
Deliverer
Desire of Nations
Despised and Rejected of
 Men
Died and Lives Again
Discerner
Dominion
Door
Dwelling Place
El Shaddai—All-Sufficient
El Elyon—Most High God
Elohim—Eternal God
Eloi—God Who Sees
Endures
Enthroned
Eternal God
Eternal Life
Ever-Present
Everlasting Father
Everlasting Name

Exalted
Excellent
Expected One
Faithful and True
Father of Lights
Father of Mercies
Father to the Fatherless
First and the Last
Firstborn of Creation
Forerunner
Forgiveness of Sin
Fortress
Foundation Stone
Fountain for Sin
Fragrance
Friend, Friend of Sinners
Full of Grace and Truth
Fullness
Generous
Gentle and Kind
Gift of God
Giver of Every Good Gift
Giver of Life
Glorious Lord
Glory of Israel
God of All Comfort
God of All Grace
God of Deliverances
God of Glory
God of Hope
God of Israel
God of Love and Peace
God of Retribution
God of Vengeance
God our Savior
God the Father
God Who Sees
Good
Good Shepherd
Governor
Grace and Gracious
Great
Great High Priest

Guard and Guardian of
    My Soul
Guarantor of a Better
    Covenant
Guide
Head of the Church
Head of Every Man
Healer
Hears
Heavenly Father
Heir of All Things
Help and Helper
Hiding Place
High and Exalted One
Holy
Holy One of Israel
Holy Spirit
Hope
Horn of Salvation
Humble
Husband
I AM
Image of God
Immanuel, Always with Us
Immortal
Incarnate
Incorruptible
Indwelling
Infinite
Inheritance
Innocent, Sinless, Perfect
Intercessor
Instructor
Jealous God
Jehovah-Jireh (Provider)
Jehovah-M'Kaddesh
    (Sanctification)
Jehovah-Nissi (Banner)
Jehovah-Rohi (Shepherd)
Jehovah-Rophe (Healer)
Jehovah-Shammah
    (Ever-Present)
Jehovah-Shalom (Peace)
Jehovah-Taidkemu
    (Righteousness)
Jesus
Jesus Christ our Lord
Jesus of Nazareth
Jesus the Son of God
Joy
Judge of all the earth

Just One and Justifier
Keeper
King Eternal
King of Glory
King of Israel
King of the Jews
King of kings
Lamb of God
Lamp
Lawgiver
Liberty
Life and Life-Giving Spirit
Light
Light of the Nations
Light of Revelation
Light of the World
Lily of the Valleys
Lion of Judah
Living Bread
Living God
Living Water, Unfailing
    Spring
Long-suffering
Lord God, the Almighty
Lord Jesus Christ
Lord of All
Lord of Glory
Lord of the Harvest
Lord of Hosts
Lord of Lords
Lord of the Sabbath
Love and Loving
Lover of My Soul
Lovingkindness
Lowly in Heart
Magnificent
Maker
Majesty, Majestic Glory
Man Christ Jesus
Man of Sorrows
Man Whom God
    Appointed
Marred, Pierced, Stricken,
    Rejected
Marvelous
Mediator
Meek
Merciful
Messiah
Mighty God
Morning Star

Most High God
Nailed to a Cross
Name Above All Names
Near
Never-Failing
New Covenant of God
None Other
Obedient Son
Offering for Sin
Omnipotent
Omnipresent
Omniscient
On High Forever
Only Begotten Son
Only God our Savior
Only One
Only Wise God
Over All
Overcomer
Paraclete
Pardons
Passover, Blood of the
    Lamb
Patient
Peace
Perfect
Physician
Portion
Potter
Power and Wisdom of God
Precious Cornerstone
Priest
Prince of Peace
Prophet
Propitiation for Our Sins
Protector
Provider
Pure and Purifier
Quieter of the Storm
Quick and Powerful Word
    of God
Quickener
Rabboni
Radiance of His Glory
Ransom
Reconciliation
Redeemer and Redemption
Refiner
Refining Fire
Refuge
Reigns

Rescuer
Restorer of My Soul
Resurrection and the Life
Revelation
Reviving One
Rewarder and Reward
Righteous One
Righteous Judge
Righteousness
Risen Lord
Rock of Salvation
Rock of Refuge and
    Strength
Root and Offspring of
    David
Rose of Sharon
Ruler
Salvation
Same
Sanctuary
Sanctification
Satisfaction
Scepter
Searches Hearts and Minds
Security
Seed of Abraham
Seeker
Sent
Servant of God
Shade
Shadow of the Almighty
Shelter
Shepherd

Shield
Sin-bearing Sacrifice
Slow to Anger
Son of David
Son of God
Son of the Highest
Son of Man
Son of Righteousness
Song
Source
Sovereign
Spirit of Adoption
Spirit of Counsel and
    Power
Spirit of the Father
Spirit of God
Spirit of Grace
Spirit of Holiness
Spirit of the Lord
Spirit of Truth
Spotless, unblemished
Stay
Steadfast
Strength
Strong Deliverer
Stronghold
Suffering Servant
Sufficient
Sun and Shield
Sun of Righteousness
Sure and our Surety
Sustainer
Teacher from God

Tower of Strength
True God
True Light
True Riches
Trustworthy
Truth
Unchanging
Understanding
Uniter
Unsearchable
Unspeakable Gift
Upholder of All Things
Upright One
Vengeance
Very Present Help
Victorious Warrior
Victory
Vindicator
Vine and Vinedresser
Voice of the Lord
Wall of Fire
Way
Witness to the Peoples
Wonderful Counselor
Word of God
Word of Life
Works Wonders
Worthy
Yahweh
Yesterday and Forever the
    Same
Zealous
Zion's Righteous King

Author

LINDA DILLOW and her husband, Jody, have lived in Europe and Asia and have been involved in international ministry for more than twenty-five years. A highly requested speaker for retreats and Bible studies, she is the author of *Intimate Issues, Intimacy Ignited* (NavPress, coauthored with Lorraine Pintus), *and A Deeper Kind of Calm* (NavPress). She and her husband now reside in Monument, Colorado. They have four grown children and are grandparents.